The Decorative Workshop

STENCILING

The Decorative Workshop

STENCILING

KATRINA HALL • LAURENCE LLEWELYN-BOWEN

FRIEDMAN/FAIRFAX
PUBLISHERS

Dedication

For all our mothers, Stephanie, Patricia, Diana and Ellen

Acknowledgments

The authors gratefully acknowledge the help of the following: Ms. Kerry Rew, Edding (UK) Ltd., Mr. Jason Da Souza, Ms. Melina Da Souza, Ms. Emma Pierce, Winsor & Newton, Borderline (Cydney Barker and Sally Baring), Mrs. Jacqeline Llewelyn-Bowen, Mrs. Stephanie Hall, Mrs. Diana Wright, Felicity Binyon, Ben and Sara Stocks, Pete Hampel, Julian Stocks, the Gilchrists, Davina Denman, Guy Butterwick, Sarah Bouchier, Serisa Hearn and Henrietta Watson.

A FRIEDMAN/FAIRFAX BOOK

Published in 1995 by Michael Friedman Publishing Group, Inc.
by arrangement with Merehurst Ltd., Ferry House, 51-57 Lacy Road
Putney, London SW1 51PR

© 1993 Merehurst Ltd

Library of Congress Cataloging-in-Publication Data

Hall, Katrina.
   [Decorative stenciling]
   Decorative workshop. Stenciling / Katrina Hall, Laurence Llewelyn-Bowen.
     p. cm.
   "Originally published as Decorative stencilling"—T.p. verso.
   Includes bibliographical references and index.
   ISBN 1-56799-210-2 (paperback)
   ISBN 1-56799-214-5 (hardcover)
   1. Stencil work. I. Llewellyn-Bowen, Laurence. II. Title.
TT270. H35 1995
745.7'3—dc20

95-12165
CIP

Editor: Miren Lopategui
Designer: Lisa Tai
Photographer: Jon Bouchier

Originally published as *Decorative Stencilling.*

Typeset by J&L Composition Ltd.
Color separations by Global Colour, Malaysia.
Printed in Singapore by C.S. Graphics.

For bulk purchases and special sales, please contact:
Friedman/Fairfax Publishers
Attention: Sales Department
15 West 26th Street
New York, NY 10010 212/685-6610 FAX 212/685-1307

Contents

Introduction

Despite changing fashions and technical improvements, stenciling—one of the most ancient design techniques—remains immensely popular with professional decorators and homeowners alike. In one form or another, it's still the technique most commonly used for producing patterns in quantity: the repeated application of paint or ink through a stiff board or template cut through with a design has created many of the world's most beautiful fabrics and wallpapers.

It's easy to understand why stenciling is so popular. Like most good ideas, it is simple—no special equipment or previous experience is necessary, and only one basic pattern is required.

There is also no end to its uses, whether for unifying the design scheme in an entire room, or adding that extra finishing touch to the most ordinary of objects in your home. You can use it on anything, ranging from the tiniest of boxes to a cushion or lampshade—even a window.

The flexibility of stenciling can be seen by a quick glance at the history of interior decoration. Over 2,000 years ago, the ancient Egyptians were already using ordered, geometric stencils to create magnificent borders in their tombs and palaces. In the tenth century A.D., the Chinese cut more intricate stencils to make dense, closely repeating patterns covering entire walls, while in thirteenth-century Europe, the jewel-like painted interiors of the Gothic cathedrals would have been impossible to achieve without the use of a stencil.

Although stenciling enjoyed a Victorian Gothic revival in England in the middle of the nineteenth century, it was in eighteenth-century America that it really became raised to an art form. Previously, stenciled finishes had been retouched to make them look more like freehand paintings, or polished up so that the final effect was closer to block-printed wallpaper. But settlers of the eighteenth-century American colonies understood that the slightly patchy, often rough finish left by the paint applied through the stencil had its own design possibilities.

The stenciled room.

Despite keeping completely abreast of European fashions, the early Americans were a three-month voyage away from the furnishings, papers and fabrics of Paris and London. So, as with their furniture styles, they reinterpreted fashionable forms and executed them with local materials and craftsmen, or, in more far-flung communities, did it all themselves. This approach and style later became known as "colonial," with regional variations such as "French Colonial" around New Orleans; "Neo Dutch" in New York; "New England" and, of course, "Shaker." However, since the Shakers—members of a strict, religious order—believed all forms of decoration to be frivolous and therefore ultimately the work of the Devil, any instances of Shaker stencils are rare.

THE PRESENT DAY

Between us we must have stenciled just about anything that can take a coat of paint, from light

fixtures to chair backs; restaurant walls to shop ceilings; glass doors to exotic floors—and even, when required by theatrical productions, an occasional naked body or two. In the commercial world, there's a strongly held belief that stenciling is a costly and difficult technique, which means that it's not often used in large commercial contracts. From experience we have found this to be completely untrue, and in fact will often deliberately choose stenciling over more popular options such as wallpaper. We have always found that by cutting and designing our own stencils, we can exercise complete control over the pattern, color and form of the decorations. When using wallpapers produced by another designer, there is obviously always the problem of fitting a scheme around their repeats and colors, which inevitably leads to unsuccessful compromises.

Used on a smaller scale in the home, stenciling really comes into its own. Unlike many other decorative techniques, it is neither time-consuming nor complicated, and provided your choice of stencil paint is compatible with the surface you are stenciling (see page 34), you can start almost immediately. Working in the commercial world, deadlines are all-important, which means that schemes must be simple in order to be done quickly. We have, therefore, ensured that all the projects in this book meet the standards of economy, simplicity and durability to which we, as professionals, have to be committed.

From the course of our work and long experience, we can say there are several golden rules to adhere to. The first is never to skimp on the early

stages. Time spent developing your stencil design and analyzing its shape, scale and "repeat" (not to mention the color scheme) will dramatically increase your chances of success.

You will soon find yourself creating stunning results with a minimum of effort, but even this tiny amount of effort will require enough commitment and seriousness to see the job through. So, if you're a first-time stenciler, start small and with a clear plan. Overestimate the time it's going to take you to complete the project, and then prepare yourself to be pleasantly surprised when you finish ahead of schedule.

Finally, don't be too easily put off. Leafing through glossy interior design magazines, it's all too easy to dismiss the elegant effects achieved by

professional designers as too expensive—or difficult —and therefore unrealistic for your purposes. By sitting down and really analyzing how the look has been achieved, you will quickly see—as we did—that even the most complicated interior designs are based upon variations of quite basic combinations of pattern, form and color.

The American settlers serve as excellent role models here. Like all of us, they must have looked at sumptuously illustrated pattern books (their equivalent of our glossy home decorating magazines) and dreamed of how wonderful it would be to have rare and beautiful patterned silks, and velvety-soft flocked wallpapers in their homes. Cost and logistics made owning the originals impossible, so they learned to achieve the same effects by cutting stencils from the fabulous patterns of the originals and then letting their imaginations run wild. With just a little flair and a bit of planning, anyone can turn their own dream scheme into reality.

Equipment and Materials

The wide range of stenciling equipment on the market provides stencilers with plenty of choices. For those who prefer special stenciling kits and paints, these are also available. They can be a real confidence boost if you are a beginner, but more ordinary materials will achieve the same effects—and are often cheaper!

Equipment and materials

IF YOU ARE STENCILING FOR THE FIRST TIME, YOU may well be tempted to go for pre-cut stencils and special paints and crayons—or even some of the complete stenciling kits that are now available in many art supply or decorating stores. This has obvious advantages, but there can be a downside, too. Ready-made kits can be expensive, and the constraints of using an inherited design can limit your creativity. And while it is true that there are many special stencil paints around—even ones that are specially designed for stenciling on fabrics, tiles and china—they often involve complicated processes using stabilizers, fixatives and the like.

It's not necessary to buy these products for successful stenciling—there can be no doubt that exactly the same effects can be easily achieved with more common materials—but for many people who are starting out, special stencil paints or crayons may understandably offer a confidence boost that overrides all other considerations. For those preferring the "do-it-yourself" approach, the main equipment to buy is as follows:

STENCIL PLATES
These fall into several types:
Oiled paper, or "oil board," is the traditional choice for stenciling. This strong, durable paper is coated with oil to make it less porous. It is available from most well-stocked art supply stores.

There is a wide variety of ready-made stencils on the market. Although handy for the beginner, they can be expensive.

Oiled paper, the traditional choice for stenciling.

Acetate has one major advantage over oiled paper. It is see-through, which makes it easy to see exactly what you are doing as you go along. This means that any dribbles or unfortunate smudges can be spotted as they occur, and dealt with before they have time to dry or harden. It's also useful when working on complicated repeating patterns or additional colors, since positioning the stencil in relation to the design can be done visually. As a plastic, acetate is the most durable stenciling material available. Like oil board, it can be bought from art supply stores. The toughness that makes acetate extremely attractive for a large stenciling project unfortunately means that it is not the most sympathetic material to cut. A sharp blade can follow even the most intricate cuts successfully, but acetate's smooth surface will make slipping blades an occupational hazard. The extra care needed in cutting is, however, offset by the advantage of being able to cut your pattern straight from the design by placing the acetate directly over the original drawing and cutting line for line. Once cut, acetate is without a doubt the best stencil for awkward corners, as it can be bent easily while remaining stiff enough to leave even the finest details intact.

Tracing paper cannot be praised enough. It has all the best properties of both acetate and oiled paper, being easily cut, translucent and extremely durable. Added to this, it has the unique and extremely useful advantage of being suitable for use in a photocopier. This means that you can have your design copied directly onto the trace. During this process, the drawing can be blown up or reduced to fit a specific space, or the image multiplied to make a repeating pattern. (If you would rather not use a photocopy machine, you can cut your pattern line for line, as with acetate.) Being thinner than oil board or acetate, tracing paper will give your finished design beautifully crisp, neat outlines. And, despite being so tough that it cannot be torn, it offers enough friction for a sharp blade to be easily controlled, thus minimizing the risk of inadvertent slipping. Larger art supply stores should stock it, and anyone listed under "graphic suppliers" in the telephone book will doubtless have some tucked away.

Above *Cutting line for line is a major advantage of both acetate and tracing paper.*

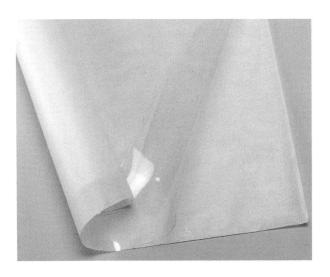

Far left *Acetate is extremely tough and durable and is much valued for commercial stenciling projects.*

Left *Tracing paper is the ideal medium for stenciling, combining the qualities of both oiled paper and acetate.*

CUTTING TOOLS

You will soon find that with the wrong equipment, cutting a stencil can be one of the most laborious, stressful and uncomfortable pursuits ever known. The only way to make the process easier is to use a sharp cutting tool. This means not only starting off with a sharp blade, but taking pains to change it regularly for a fresh one the minute cutting your stencil becomes heavy going. Beyond that, the choice of blade holder is a matter of personal comfort. Obviously, large craft or utility knives with their thick blades, while ideal for consistent straight cuts, are not suited to intricate patterns. Of the multitude of other craft knives available, the best are usually those which can be comfortably held like a pen. The best knives on the market are X-Acto knives, round-shafted knives with replaceable blades. These are comfortable to use and are perfect for cutting tight corners and sharp details. The next step down would be the flat-handled craft knives with retractable, disposable blades. They can, however, be as unwieldy as the larger knives,

Of the wide variety of craft knives available, X-Acto knives are the best suited for stenciling projects.

with the added disadvantage of small blades that break easily under sideways pressure. It is at the lower end of the market that you will find the most flexible cutting tool.

X-Acto knife Once you have conquered your initial shock at wielding such a frighteningly surgical implement, you will find that the long, graceful blade is a joy to steer. X-Acto knives come in a range of shapes and sizes. Convex or concave blades are not appropriate for cutting stencils. Opt instead for the medium to fine straight-edged blades. Consult the sales assistant before committing yourself, however, since various blades are designed to fit specific handles, and no amount of tape will make a large blade firm on a small handle.

Scissors There are some patterns, such as simple star shapes or large flowing designs, where sharp, pointed scissors can be used successfully. The shock given to the stencil when cutting can, however, make permanent creases that will make using the stencil difficult. Scissors are not nearly as easy to control as a knife and can make it difficult to see the line as you are cutting.

Pinking shears can be used to create a decorative saw-toothed edge. They are really only at their best, however, when used for long, straight runs. The relative smallness of the zigzag edge can look just plain messy when seen from a distance, but for smaller objects seen at close range, they can offer some interesting stenciled effects.

PAINTS

Having already covered paints specially made for stenciling, an investigation into less costly and more widely available alternatives should be considered.

Latex Ordinary household latex paint has much to recommend it in that it's easy to get hold of and offers an almost infinite choice of colors. Latex is a water-soluble paint and as such is easy to handle

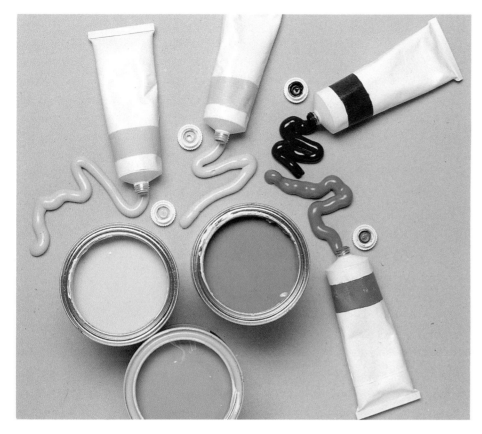

Left Household latex paint is available in several finishes, including eggshell, semi-gloss, and flat.

Below Stenciling a design in eggshell onto a flat base of the same color.

Stenciling projects can be undertaken with household latex paint or artist's acrylic paints, as shown here.

and not difficult to remove from brushes, provided they are rinsed immediately after use. It offers several finishes, including flat and eggshell. The former gives a surface similar to old-fashioned "distemper" without the unstable powdery chalkiness; the latter leaves a similar effect to traditional oil paints with their discreet sheen. Many companies produce latex in very small containers as color testers, which are an ideal size for most stenciling projects.

Stenciling with latex, whether eggshell or flat, can be a little tricky to begin with. Applying paint straight from the container will doubtless mean you end up forcing too much paint through the stencil, leaving a smudged and messy pattern not readily recognizable even to its own designer. The simple solution is to call into play the paint "reservoir" (see page 19). Given this means of regulating the paint flow, many interesting effects can be achieved by off-setting eggshell against flat latex. Stenciling a design in a slightly darker shade of eggshell onto a flat base of the same color can give you effects similar to rich damasks or brocades. Alternatively, by isolating and stenciling one element in eggshell, you can lend an exciting feeling of movement to the overall design as the light is reflected by the paint's slight sheen.

Artist's acrylic paints From experience, acrylic is the most flexible and manageable option. All art supply stores now stock acrylic paints, since they have to a large extent overtaken the former popularity of oil paints among amateur artists. When standing in your local art supply store confronted by a variety of paint displays, you will normally find at least four types of paint on sale: oil, acrylic, alkyd and gouache. Sometimes alkyd, acrylic and gouache get mixed up, so make sure you don't leave the store with a tube or pot of gouache

Artist's acrylic paints come in a wide variety of stunning colors.

or any other paint referred to as "watercolor" or "poster paint." Not only are these paints water-soluble, they will remain so after you have finished the project.

Following years of research, acrylic paints are now manufactured to be immensely durable and fade-resistant, and come in a staggering range of colors, including fluorescent, pearlescent and metallic finishes. The main advantage of using acrylics for stenciling is that you can control the paint's consistency and texture straight from the tube. Undiluted, acrylic paint is much "harder" and "drier" than latex and can be used to create interesting textured finishes with a brush or sponge. You will find that it dries almost instantly on the wall. This has the advantage of minimizing the risk of damaging your design when moving your stencil, but inevitably means that smudges and other mistakes are impossible to remove. For more subtle, slightly transparent effects, a little water in the mixture will soften the finish. Be warned that acrylic's fast-drying properties can have disastrous and irreparable effects on brushes and sponges left out of water.

Acrylic paints are not generally produced in the subtle shades most of us like to use in home decoration. You will therefore have to be prepared to mix colors to achieve the right hue (see pp. 32–33). Unfortunately, the cost of using acrylics can mount up, since you may have to buy several tubes of paint to achieve the right shade.

Alkyd paints have been formulated to provide many of the qualities of oil paints, with as rapid a drying time as that of acrylic. Alkyd colors are thinned with mineral spirits or turpentine, which is necessary to make their "buttery" texture suitable for stenciling.

Oil paints For the purist or revivalist, there can be no choice other than oil paints. They are, however, the trickiest paint to use for stenciling and dry extremely slowly. For those who have mastered how to apply them and have a good idea of the ideal paint consistency for stenciling, oil paint mixed with a little varnish or oil painting medium can be used to create beautiful transparent effects. Extreme care must be taken in removing the stencil after applying paint, however, since oil pigments remain unstable for a minimum of four hours, which could lead to smudges if you are clumsy. (Any such horrors can be easily "erased" with a clean rag or cotton ball, however, as long as the mistake is small and close to an element of the design with which you are happy.) Unlike other paints, oils can be used on nearly every surface except the obvious paint repellers such as laminates, glass, ceramics and unprimed metals. You won't find

Artist's oil paints are ideal for subtle or earthy tones.

Far left As yet, the choice of colors available in spray paints is limited. Mixing colors can be achieved with successive sprays.

Left Masking the area around the stencil is essential to prevent the spray from hitting areas nearby.

many of the bright colors offered by acrylics, but for mellow earth tones or smoky shades, they are difficult to beat. As with acrylic, building up a palette of colors with them can be costly.

Spray paints A comparatively recent addition to the stenciler's armory, spray paints are ideal for those who find hand-applied methods difficult to master. So-called "craft sprays" are available from art, craft and model shops in an increasing but still limited color range. While these are appropriate for most surfaces, you may need to call upon the impregnable finish offered by car sprays if you want to stencil on surfaces such as glass, ceramics or metals. Even then, car sprays are not recommended for use on objects that are cleaned regularly or that get heavy wear. Of all the paints discussed, car sprays have the most limited color range. They are also highly toxic and must be used only under well ventilated conditions and with a face mask. Inhaling deeply in a closed room where car spray has just been used will give your lungs a very good idea of how the ozone layer feels.

Whether using a car spray or craft spray, you must be careful to spray a very fine layer—almost a dusting—through the stencil. Applying too much paint will lead to immediate runs and dribbles—a

particular hazard with car spray, which has a long hardening or drying time. The only way of achieving a light paint layer is to hold the can as far from the stencil as possible. This, of course, means that you run the risk of spraying not only through the stencil but around the stencil as well. It's a good idea in such cases to mask the area around the stencil with scrap paper. This is not difficult and will prove invaluable in protecting adjacent finishes.

The only way to mix spray colors is to use successive, very lightly sprayed coats of paint. Since the paint hits the wall in minute pinprick spots, it is by offsetting one color spot against another that different hues are achieved, just like a television screen, where all the colors are created by differing densities of tiny red, green and blue dots.

Finally, for those whose commitment to the environment forbids the propulsion of paint courtesy of CFCs, there are do-it-yourself spray alternatives. For example, some artist's airbrushes are ideal for stenciling, though they can be quite expensive. They create a gentle, focused spray that is excellent for intricate or delicate stencils, or for subtle gradations of color.

Colour mixing with spray paint, when looked at close up, closely resembles the spots of color on a television screen.

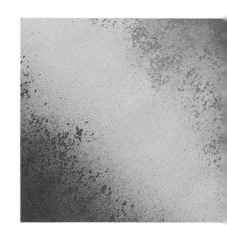

PAINT APPLICATORS

Applying any kind of paint through a stencil using a small sponge applicator (see page 19) has many advantages—it is quick, cheap and disposable. The problem with an applicator, however, is that it will not give you the same control or offer such a wide variety of effects as a brush.

Brushes specifically designed for stenciling have short, stiff hairs. Available from art supply stores and craft shops, they can also sometimes be found in hardware or paint stores. As befits such specialized tools, stencil brushes constitute one of the biggest financial commitments for the stenciler. It is possible, however, to use ordinary decorator's paintbrushes: 1-inch (2.5cm), 2-inch (5cm) and 3-inch (7.5cm) brushes are best. Man-made bristles are less flexible than exotic, luxuriously soft badger hair and work better.

Nothing beats a proper stencil brush, but you can adapt an ordinary brush to make it more efficient, by binding the brush or cutting it down (see below).

As a finishing touch, a rag or sponge dipped in drying paint will give a direct imprint that can be used as an interesting random effect over a more opaque application of color.

RUBBER GLOVES

Whatever your chosen technique, stenciling has the unfortunate side effect of leaving as much pigment on your hands as on the wall. So, unless you're prepared to spend the next week with permanently painted fingers, you are advised to wear rubber gloves when applying the paint. Standard household rubber gloves, however, can be very cumbersome. The best alternative is surgical gloves, which can be purchased from any medical supplier.

Stenciling brushes have characteristically short, stubby hairs. Though not ideal, ordinary household brushes can be adapted to meet these needs.

Tightly bind a strip of masking tape about a third of the way down the bristles to make them stiff.

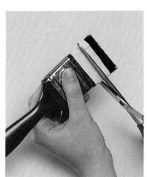

Or, bind the bristles as above, then cut the bristles by cutting through the tape.

Making your own paint applicator

Your own paint applicator can be made from a small square pad cut from an ordinary synthetic sponge—the large, Swiss cheese-like holes of natural sponges will cause a disastrous buildup of paint. Simply cut off about one-third to one-half of the sponge, depending on your design, and keep the rest to use as a paint "reservoir." Paint reservoirs act like ink pads to help solve a major problem when stenciling: irregular flow of paint through the stencil. It's important to get this right.

Too much paint, and the design will smudge; too little, and you will have only faint patterns.

To prepare the paint, mix a tiny amount of water with some latex paint in an old saucer (you can easily soak the paint off later with detergent and hot water), then squeeze the reservoir sponge firmly into the paint until it has taken up most of the mixture. Gently dab with a small pad cut from the remaining sponge onto the reservoir until this, too, has taken up the paint. Then dab it again on a clean sheet of newspaper or an uncut part of the stencil, to check that the paint isn't oozing or dribbling. A clean, crisp imprint of the sponge means that you are ready to start stenciling. You can then continue to use your applicator to paint your stencil, building up the density of paint as you go along, and following the techniques described on page 34.

Pour latex into a saucer, covering it by about one-third. Add a dribble of water and gently mix together, then squeeze the reservoir sponge firmly into the paint until it has taken up most of the mixture. Dab the smaller applicator sponge onto the reservoir until this, too, has taken up the paint. Then use the applicator to paint the stencil.

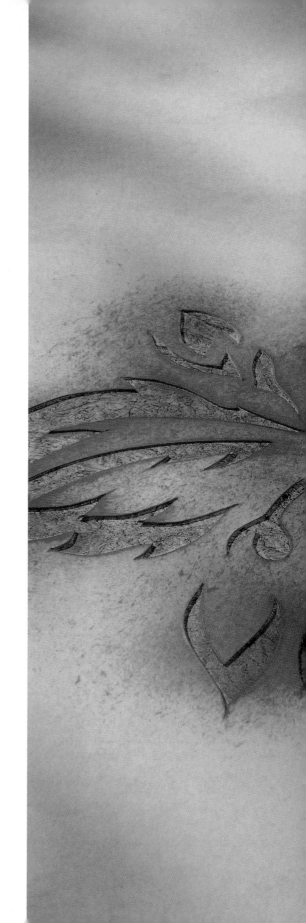

Techniques

Decorative stenciling techniques are easy to master and, once learned, will serve as a springboard to help you create your own patterns and motifs. There may be a great deal of planning and preparation in the initial stages, but the net result—a unique and individually conceived design—will be infinitely more rewarding than anything you can ever buy in a store!

Designing your stencil

IT'S NOW TIME TO START MAKING SOME BIG decisions. At this stage, you will probably have an exact image of the finished project in your mind. But, inevitably, it's transforming this abstract idea into reality that, for many beginners and professionals alike, is one of the most daunting parts of the whole stenciling process.

First, think of the specific job you want your stencil design to do. One of the most effective uses of stenciling is to provide "accents" of pattern or color that can bridge a gap between, say, your curtain fabric or upholstery and other elements in the room. You can do this by repeating an existing pattern on objects such as lampshades or mirror frames, or with repeated details running around the perimeter of a room, as in a frieze or dado.

If you are a beginner, the simplest and most direct starting point may be to "lift" a design element that is already in your room—say, the curtains, or a cushion or seat cover—by tracing it. When dealing with a large free-form "repeat" with a variety of contrasting elements, this can seem daunting. So begin by flattening the design —draw the curtains, squeeze all the air from the cushion, or remove the stuffing from the seat covers.

Having done this, stand back as far away from the pattern as space will allow and squint your eyes until the overall design becomes a blur. You will soon notice some elements in the design are stronger and more dominant than others—perhaps because of the way they are drawn, the strength or

For most people, the first step in creating their own stencil is to carefully trace the pattern of a fabric or wallpaper they already have in their home.

After tracing the design, the next step is to take out any small, detailed or complicated shapes that might prove impossible to reproduce. Your aim should be to create a design that, while obviously derived from the original, uses only the most important shape.

depth of the color used, or the darkness or "tonal value" of the motif. It is these dominant elements that will provide the framework for your pattern.

Once you have done this, you will then need to do some further editing, depending on the stenciling projects you have planned. A single pattern, such as an isolated motif on, say, a chair seat or tray, is simple to start with; as long as the scale is right, the motif won't need much reworking. If, on the other hand, you want to tackle a repeating stencil to border your room or a lampshade, it's best to focus on an element that spreads to either side of the design. Leaves or scrolls that stick out from a more densely patterned center will give you more leeway to link the space between each repeat. A nicely framed flower or a symmetric element that leans heavily to one side, on the other hand, will be very difficult to repeat without adding other linking elements taken from either the overall pattern or your own imagination.

TRACING THE DESIGN

Having chosen the starting point of your design, flatten out the pattern and trace it out accurately line for line. Bear in mind that a felt-tip pen or a very soft pencil is easier to maneuver on fabric than the spearlike points of ballpoint pens or hard pencils. Permanent markers may bleed through tracing paper, so use them carefully. At this early stage, you may find yourself tracing a pattern several times to get the best outline, since it's inevitable that the tracing paper and traced pattern will move as you draw, causing distortions in the design. You may find it helpful to include surrounding elements in your trace, even though at first glance they don't seem appropriate for inclusion. They may well prove useful as the design evolves.

Taking your carefully copied design, sit down and think about how it can be simplified. Analyze its overall shape and its most dominant elements.

Then take another sheet of tracing paper and make a new copy, leaving out any smaller detailed elements that might be impossible to reproduce. Your goal should be to create a design that, while obviously derived from the original, uses only the broader, flatter and more important shapes. For instance, a curving tendril of ivy, complete with stalk and runners in the original, can be effectively mirrored by simply concentrating on the broad, pointed shapes of the leaves while completely ignoring the fine details that have been used to define the stalk. As long as the leaves are positioned accurately, the gentle curve of the motif will still be maintained even without the extra detail.

NEGATIVE AND POSITIVE SPACE

You will now need to look at your traced design with a critical eye as to its practicality as a stencil. Most stencils use "negative space"—that is, it's the bit you cut out that creates the pattern. Obviously, that negative space must be completely surrounded by positive space—the uncut remainder of the stencil—so, focusing on each element, check that your design is surrounded by a constant border that will not be cut or broken by the intrusion of another shape. This is where you will have to start

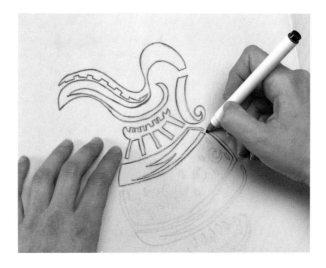

Using a medium to thick marker, draw around the design to outline the areas that you will be cutting.

creating your own borders of "bridges," or "filaments," to define a pattern. On a luscious bunch of grapes that in the original was given shape and form by different colors, you will have to rely on creating a filament that defines the shape of each grape. For something this detailed, think again about its suitability for your project. You may find that the same effect can be achieved by outlining the entire bunch and then defining the space between just a few of the grapes. The same applies to more complicated flower or leaf shapes. For your stencil to work properly, you will need a space of around ¼ inch (5mm) between each cut. Smaller bridges will not only break easily, but can also allow paint to seep behind the stencil. Always try to avoid leaving too many floating bridges. Just being joined at one end can make the bridge wobbly enough to move as you apply the paint, or cause it to become creased as you remove the stencil.

Having made sure that each negative space is constantly bordered by the positive, start mapping out where you want your bridges. By far the easiest way of proceeding is to follow the design line for line with an extremely thick marker pen. A wide nib will give you the thickness of each bridge in one line, but make a mental note that when it comes to cutting, you must cut on either side of the line rather than down the middle.

SCALING UP AND DOWN

It's now time to try the design and see how it looks in its final resting place. You may discover that it is too small or too big. This is very easy to solve with a quick trip to the nearest photocopier. Just take a ruler and measure the correct size you want your motif to be enlarged or reduced to. Photocopiers work on a rather complicated system of pre-set percentages, and you may find that you have to accept a copy that is not the exact measurement you wanted. Don't worry about this. It's very rare that a slightly undersized or

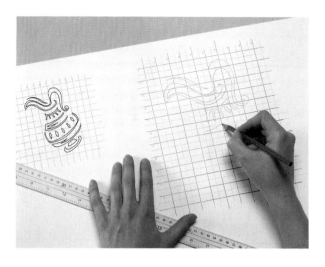

To double the size of any motif, draw a grid over the original. Then, by drawing another grid exactly twice the size of the first, you can transfer the design line for line using the squares as a point of reference.

oversized stencil doesn't work as well as one with the correct dimensions. Always have one or two copies made that are both larger and smaller than the correct size, and keep any intermediate-sized copies, as you may find them useful later. Also, have a handful of copies made of the right size so that you can play around with them when you get home, refining some shapes, eliminating others and trying out different color combinations.

If photocopiers intimidate you, there's another technique you can use for scaling up or down. This will involve a grid. If, for example, your original is 8 inches (20cm) high and your finished stencil needs to be 16 inches (40cm) to fit comfortably on the surface you have prepared, draw a grid over the original with squares that measure 1 × 1 inch (2.5 × 2.5cm). On a separate sheet of paper draw another grid, each of whose squares is exactly double, that is 2 × 2 inches (5 × 5cm). It will help if you draw the grid in ink, since you'll have to transfer the design freehand from grid to grid, rubbing out mistakes. Then, with or without a ruler, assess the position of each line within the square. A line that cuts a square diagonally from corner to corner in the original can then be easily reproduced on the larger grid. Always start off by sketching in the overall shape of the pattern, leaving any details until later. Go for simplified, perhaps even squared off, lines at first. You can always give them a more accurate shape later.

You are now left with the bare bones of your stencil. It's always a good idea to give yourself some time at this stage. Stick the stencil design in its intended position, and use a critical eye to see how well it's going to work. During the early stages of simplification, your design may have been left looking a little sparse. Or, it may not have the right shape or outline for the intended effect. If your stencil is to repeat, now is the time to place two or three copies close together to see how the overall design will work. Tightening up your design now will require a little creativity, and you may have to resort to basic collage skills learned in elementary school. If you find you have a particularly noticeable blank space, rummage through the earlier stages of your design, paying particular attention to the photocopies you made that were under- or oversized. The first-stage design should also be considered, with particular thought given to the elements bordering the design in the original pattern. Cut out anything you feel may be useful, and play around with your new-found palette of pattern elements. You'll be surprised at the results. What may have been an oversized vine leaf when you started out could now, through the expediencies of scale, fit exactly in an unsightly blank space. If you come across an element that's both the right size and the right shape but pointing in the wrong direction, don't forget that tracing it and reversing the paper will give you an exact mirror image. You might even find yourself returning to the original at this stage to find additional elements to pep up the design. When you have the effect you want, get out the glue and stick your design down onto paper.

It is now time to make the final copy. You could always photocopy the pasteup and leave it at that, but a fresh trace is a good idea, to keep the lines nice and clean, and to help you refine the design further.

To finalize any design, reassembling extra pieces or unwanted preliminary drawings will help in filling blank spaces or balancing the look of the motif.

Experienced stencilers know the value of a clean-lined final design to follow when cutting the stencil. This is best achieved by making a final trace of the design.

Clean, flowing lines are normally a sign of confidence; an insecure draftsman tends to draw lines in small, broken strokes, particularly if using a hard pencil or ballpoint pen. If you feel apprehensive, it may help to make a tracing of your design with a very soft pencil, felt-tip pen or small watercolor brush dipped in ink. By using tracing paper, you won't be marking or damaging the original and can therefore allow yourself to loosen up. If you make a mess, all you need do is start again on a new trace. As you build up speed and confidence, you will find that not only will the lines become more constant, but the design will start to achieve a flowing elegance that did not come across with your original disjointed pencil marks. For smaller, more intricate or detailed parts of the design, you will obviously need a sharper line. Even here, however, try, if possible, to use one line per element.

You now have your final design or, as it was known in the Renaissance, "cartoon." One of the advantages of tracing paper is that you can now look at its mirror image by turning the paper over—an old trick used by the Italian painters. By doing this, anything that doesn't quite come off will be much more apparent.

TRANSFERRING THE DESIGN

The final design is now ready for another trip to the photocopier. This is not essential, but can offer valuable insurance if the worst should happen during the cutting process. If tracing paper is your chosen stencil medium, you can transfer the design straight onto a sheet at this stage via the photocopier. For those using acetate or tracing paper, the original should now be firmly positioned under the stencil and cutting commenced line for line. If transferring your design onto oil board, there are four methods you can use. The first is to draw a grid similar to that described earlier for rescaling the design. This means redrawing the design more or less freehand, but with a grid to give you the

essential points of reference. This inevitably leads to fuzzy lines, which you will curse when it comes to cutting, but going over the first pencil lines with a heavy felt-tip will help.

The second method, though labor-intensive, is great fun and interesting, in that it was the favored method during the Italian Renaissance. To follow in Leonardo da Vinci's footsteps, you will need to follow each line of your design with a series of pinpricks, pushing holes through the design onto a separate piece of paper. You will need to judge the distance between the holes carefully. Too far apart, and they will only leave slight impressions. Too close, and you will end up perforating the

By following the lines of a design with a pushpin and pricking through onto the stencil, you will be able to subsequently cut the lines with a knife.

design like a book of stamps. Needles and pins tend to be too fine for this exercise; pushpins, with their stout heads and long, sharp points, make the best, neatly rounded holes. Provided both design and paper are well anchored together, you can then prick your design straight through onto the paper. A more faithful transfer can be achieved by rubbing charcoal through the pinpricks onto the paper below—use a cotton ball to really force the powdery charcoal through. This method is ideal if you want to repeat the design, because any number of transfers can be made with the minimal effort required to apply the charcoal.

For most people, the simplest technique is to liberally shade the back of the design with a very soft pencil and then trace the design with a harder pencil or a ballpoint pen. On darker paper this kind of pencil transfer can be a little difficult to see, and you may have to resort to carbon or transfer paper, which will give you a nice crisp and easy-to-see line.

With all these methods, and indeed the earlier tracing stages, always make sure that neither the design nor the trace can move and distort the image. Also, make sure the tape, glue or pins you are using to keep the two elements together are easy to remove and will not mark, tear or damage the surface.

Charcoal rubbed through the holes pricked on the design will create an exact trace of the original.

Carbon or transfer paper gives the most direct impression of the original design.

Cutting the stencil

WHEN YOU HAVE TRANSFERRED THE DESIGN onto your chosen medium, you are ready to cut. The ideal surface for cutting a stencil is a self-healing cutting mat—obviously, since cutting through heavy paper, you are more than likely to cut the surface underneath. Cutting mats can be expensive, however, and adequate substitutes might include vinyl floor tiles, the underside of rubber-backed carpet tiles, heavy cardboard or the covers of unwanted books. Start with intricate shapes, since cutting these tends to pull at the paper. If you start with long or flat areas, you may find that long filaments will distort or even tear as you cut adjacent small sections. A helpful tip is to stick the paper to the cutting surface with spray adhesive before starting. It's generally a lot easier to cut towards yourself and, provided that you keep your knife as close to upright as possible, you are unlikely to slip and inadvertently commit hara-kiri. Always keep your free hand behind the cutting blade if you want to steady the stencil. Some longer lines are best cut if the knife is kept in a constant position and the stencil is moved. You will find this makes the process much less tiring and increases the flow of curved lines. Don't feel that each shape needs to be cut exactly as drawn—short cuts within the shape minimize effort. With a sharp blade, you should need to exert only minimal pressure. If you find yourself having to attack the stencil with great force, it probably means your blade has become blunt and needs to be changed.

Smaller, thinner handles will inevitably become uncomfortable after a while. A good tip is to increase the size of the handle with a liberal

For curved or flowing shapes, keeping the blade steady while moving the card will give a more consistent cut.

Knife handles can become uncomfortable. In such cases, adding masking tape will increase the size of the handle, making it easier to hold.

*Mend broken filaments
with a piece of masking tape
cut to fit the damaged area.*

wrapping of masking tape. Not only will this make the knife easier to hold, it will also give you a softer handle. Take care not to bind the blade to the handle, since you will have to be able to change your blade when necessary.

Having cut the design into the stencil, cut the stencil itself down to a more usable size. If the design is to fit a specific area, it's a good idea to cut the stencil to fit exactly. For a repeating border underneath a picture rail or cornice, the top edge of the stencil must be exactly square to keep the design from wobbling as you follow the bottom edge of the molding. Marking the middle line of the stencil will make it much easier to position. Regardless of the shape of the design, draw a square with a ruler around the motif. By joining each corner diagonally, you will find the exact center of the design where the lines meet. Using a triangle or anything you know to be a true right angle, you can then mark off the vertical midline and horizontal midline.

If the design is for a repeating border, tracing one-half of each of the neighboring motifs on either side of the stencil will help in lining up the stencil as you apply the paint. Broken or damaged filaments, or filaments accidentally sliced through as you cut, can be mended with masking tape. Making a rough or oversized splint with the tape and then cutting the masking tape down to fit will ensure that you don't break the outlines around the damaged design.

Using color

WITHOUT WISHING TO FRIGHTEN, UPSET OR PUT you off, all your hard work will be in vain if the color is not right. It's important to remember that stenciling as a decorative technique gives a fundamentally flat finish. Simple, often harsh outlines can become simpler and definitely harsher if the stencil and base colors offer too strong a contrast. The most successful stencils are without a doubt the subtler ones in which the design is applied in a color closely related to surrounding paint finishes. There can be no doubt that stenciling looks best over a mellowed paint finish. This will immediately remove any anticipated problems of harshness and ensure that your stencil doesn't end up looking as unsightly as a badly executed tattoo.

In an existing room scheme, you will have a good idea of a color you wish to either match or complement. Whatever your chosen stencil paint, it's always advisable to find the chosen color on a paint manufacturer's chart or card. Even when

The texture of objects can drastically affect the way a color looks.

The three "primary colors"—red, yellow and blue—can be arranged in a wheel. The area between each primary then provides "secondary colors"; for example, yellow mixed with blue creates green, and so on.

mixing your own colors, you will still find this point of reference extremely useful.

TAKING A COLOR DIRECTLY FROM AN EXISTING PATTERN

Above all, remember that a color in, say, a fabric or carpet has infinite variations as the light and shade hit each thread. What may appear a beautiful subtle old rose on a curtain can often turn out to be shocking pink as a painted finish. This is because the flat surface of the paint will reflect light uniformly, whereas the comparatively rough surface of fabric or even wallpaper disrupts reflection, thereby mellowing the color. It is therefore a very good idea, having matched the exact pink from your curtains, to use a shade that is, in fact, several degrees lighter. This is very easy to do from a paint chart or color card where different strengths of the same color are given.

Having said a "lighter color," it is, in fact, far more complicated than that, as your chosen lighter pink will not be the same pink as the curtains but will have added white. The subtle shades used in interior decoration achieve their subtlety from a surprising mix of colors. So, the nicest pinks are rarely just red and white but can also include, say, blue or orange.

COMPLEMENTARY COLORS

Over the last thousand years, artists have striven ceaselessly to produce naturalistic representations of colors in painting. But what appears to be a green leaf will, in fact, be made up of a variety of other hues from the yellows to blues and reds. By analyzing the colors of natural objects and the way they appear to change in different lights, the theory of "complementary colors" was evolved. This basically means that every single color has an exact opposite.

There are three key or "primary colors" from which every color can be mixed: red, yellow and blue. Different degrees of each color produce a multiplicity of shades, starting with the "secondary colors," such as green and purple. These colors are created when each primary color overlaps the other. So, thinking in terms of a rainbow, the area where red overlaps yellow becomes orange; yellow overlaps blue and becomes green, and blue overlaps red and becomes purple. As can be seen, the relationships are circular, starting at red and finishing at red, leaving what is known as the "color wheel" (see illustration). Seeing colors as a wheel, color theorists then noticed that each color had an opposite. Thus red's opposite is green, blue's opposite is orange and so on. Armed with this knowledge, understanding the intensity of colors becomes much easier. Some paint manufacturers will actually detail these relationships on their color cards, showing you, through an arrangement of letters and numbers for each paint's number, how much blue is in a green or how much yellow is in an orange. What is surprising is how much of a color's opposite or complementary hue has been used to achieve the desired shade.

Back to the pink. The real subtlety of our shade is due to the addition of red's complementary color, green. Not only does this darken the color, but it removes any harshness from the red. Theoretically, in perfectly balanced proportions, all complementary colors when mixed will achieve a uniform brown-gray. But, used sparingly, they're the best way of controlling the original color.

When talking about color, the terms "hue" and "tone" should be defined. Color refers literally to the color as in its primary or secondary name, for example, red. "Hue" defines its balance, in terms of which other color predominates, thus, a red with an orange hue would be a salmon pink. "Tone" refers to how dark it is. Assessing the hue and tone of a color can be difficult with all the distractions of a busy and highly colored pattern. You can make a good start by isolating the color to be matched with a frame of white paper. From this you will be able to see that your pink does indeed have not only a dash of orange but also the faintest suggestion of green.

When matching or evaluating a color from an existing pattern, it's often a good idea to isolate the area with a white frame to block out adjacent motifs.

MIXING COLORS

One of the biggest misconceptions is that neither black nor white are colors. True, used straight from the container, they come across as a pure or dead flat finish. But when mixed in with other colors, they will give a particular hue to the final mix that is derived from their original color balance. Blacks can, for example, vary from brown to blue to green, whites from yellow to blue. This may all sound like nit-picking but, when you're trying to mix a particular color—say, our pink—adding some blue-black to darken it may completely destroy the subtle balance of orange, red and yellow. By the same token, lightening a color with pure blue-white can overturn the established relationships and make the color too chalky or even dingy. Some guidance is given on paint tubes. For example, "Flake White" has a pinkish hue, whereas "Titanium White" is quite blue. "Lamp Black" can be rather blue-green, and "Ivory Black" is very brown. Therefore Flake White would be ideal for lightening our pink, which is very warm, and Ivory Black perfect to make it darker.

Mixing colors, like making the best pastry or the most successful mayonnaise, should be done slowly, and all the ingredients added gradually and mixed thoroughly before more is put in. A little water in acrylics and a little turpentine in oil will keep the paint pliable and easy to mix. A stiff brush is best, as it will allow you to thoroughly move the paint around. Always mix more than you need; remixing is incredibly difficult, and provided that the mixed paint is sealed with plastic wrap, you will find it will last for as long as you need it. When mixing paints, use wide bowls with low sides, to minimize shadow and allow you to see more of your mixture in direct light.

When you feel good about the color and relatively happy about the hue—perhaps having added a dash of the color's complement to keep the whole thing subtle—you must assess the tone. If your pink is now too dark for the effect you want, squeeze out some Flake White on a separate saucer or dish and to this add a little red. This will leave you with a mixture that is unlikely to upset the careful balance. Keep the new pigment quite wet and apply a dribble at a time. The same principle is applied to making the color darker with black. Whatever your chosen technique, now is the time to step back, since all paints change color from wet to dry. So, before committing yourself to your mixture, allow a small sample patch to dry fully. A small blob next to the desired color on your paint chart is ideal.

Even paints straight from the container may not be as exciting in reality as they appeared on the chart. A couple of brush strokes on a piece of paper

Whites and blacks always have a strong color bias, which can affect the final hue when mixing colors from scratch.

Colors should always be mixed in wide bowls with low sides that will not cast shadows on the mixture.

Whether mixing from scratch or tinting commercial paints, color should be added slowly and mixed vigorously as you go along.

stuck to the stencil's final destination will give you a useful opportunity to make sure it is right. Tinting paints in the container is not difficult and should be tackled using the same principles as mixing from scratch. Mix a runny version of your tint and gradually add this to the paint, mixing slowly as you go. You may find that trickling the tint down the inside of the tin will give you more flexibility and is easier to mix in than a huge blob right in the middle. It also means that you'll be left with a reservoir from which you can take small quantities. There is always a tremendous temptation to add the paint too quickly, since it's often only after subsequent mixings that the color takes. Patience is definitely a virtue in this instance. As insurance, it is always a good idea to empty an approximate third from the container just in case your mixing is heavy-handed to start with. By feeding in some of the original color you have saved gradually, most mistakes can be rectified. When in your local paint store, resist the temptation to walk out with ready-mixed tints. They are extremely strong and have ruined more paint in the hands of the impatient than can be imagined.

Most paints, whether oil, acrylic or latex, can be saved by pouring the mixed color into an airtight container, such as any kitchen jar with a lid. With your own mixed colors, an airtight lid of plastic wrap will mean you can use the paint again, though you will have to be prepared to remove any hardened paint that has formed.

If you have been a conscientious stenciler so far, you will have kept a few of the photocopies you made of the final design. You can now color these in with your chosen paint. Armed with a facsimile of the finished design, hold it as close as you can to its final position. Then, by standing back and taking stock, you can make sure you are happy with the final effect, which is an exercise well worth the effort.

Applying the stencil

FOR YOUR STENCILED SCHEME TO ENJOY A long and happy existence, it's important to assess the suitability of the surface to be stenciled. Water-based paints will never adhere properly to an oil-based surface. Though you might be able to coax them to give you a flattish finish, particularly after vigorous rubbing with heavy-duty sandpaper, they will be extremely susceptible to any kind of wear. Oil paint, however, loves nothing more than to be applied directly to surfaces primed with water-soluble latex paints.

Whatever the technique, it's always a good idea to finish off with a coat or two of varnish to create a tough protective shell. Being such a good shield, varnish is obviously one of the worst surfaces to paint on.

Latex—either flat or eggshell—is the most popular paint finish for walls. Being water-based, it will be only too happy to receive a stencil in any paint finish.

Oil-based paint, sold in a flat, eggshell, semi-gloss or gloss finish, is used for doors, windows and other woodwork. Much tougher than latex, it is designed to form a smooth surface to which dirt and water-based paint cannot cling. Craft spray, car spray or oil paint are therefore the only practical choices for stenciling on surfaces coated with oil paint.

Stenciling on varnished wood is best attempted with craft or car spray, though oil paint can work if you gently sand the surface to give the paint a rougher texture on which to cling, and do a very thorough varnishing afterward to protect it. Bare wood will take any technique. A final coat of varnish will not only make it tougher, it will also add depth to the design.

Stencils can look very effective applied directly onto wallpaper, particularly as a lacy border below a picture rail or a cresting just above a dado. Old-fashioned wallpaper will take all stenciling techniques, though vinyl wallcoverings, with their slippery coated surfaces, will quickly repel just about anything you put on them. Kitchen or bathroom tiles and laminated surfaces, though

"Broken" color is a perfect background for stenciling. Color thinned with water or varnish and rubbed with a dry rag creates a mellow texture.

Far right *On large areas such as walls, always leave a small gap between painted patches, which you can then fill in by bringing wet paint across on the rag to join the edges.*

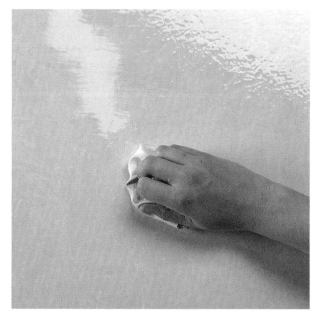

easy to stencil with the sprays, will eventually repel any paint you put on and chip and flake at the slightest knock.

PREPARING YOUR SURFACES

Before stenciling, always make sure that the surface you are going to apply the stencil to is clean and free of dust. Any project will profit from a little time spent gently sanding down the surface with some fine sandpaper. This is particularly important if you are stenciling directly onto varnish or gloss paint. Holes, cracks or irregularities should be filled and smoothed if you want a truly professional finish. However, the bumpy, time-mellowed texture of old cottage walls can add pleasing rustic elements to an appropriate stencil scheme, provided the paint is not loose or flaky.

If you are not stenciling directly onto an existing surface but want to create your own colored base, you must resign yourself to several time-consuming and thin coats. Trying to get it all done in one thick layer simply will not work. Always allow time for one coat to dry before applying the next, or else you will find that the new wet paint removes previous layers as you go along.

Stenciling is always beautifully offset by a slightly clouded paint effect used as a base. This is fairly easy to do and, in simple terms, means thinning down your paint and applying it unevenly with broad strokes from a large paintbrush, then rubbing it with a dry cloth.

Latex thinned with water can be extremely messy, so protect anything you don't want to break out in a rash of paint spots. It can also be a little tricky on a large wall, since you will find areas of the paint drying before you have time to get to them with your cloth. So restrict yourself to working in approximate 3-foot (90cm) squares, taking care not to let the paint squares overlap, since this will leave you with a darker ridge. Try leaving a small gap as you paint, then quickly filling it in by bringing the two edges together with a rag and rubbing and smudging them in. This is a very quick antidote to a brightly colored wall or other surface. A milky white or cream wash can turn intense primary colors into more muted, restrained tones.

On oil-painted surfaces, some oil pigment or paint in varnish will give you even more flexibility for exciting effects. You will find that the longer drying time of the varnish will allow you to really move the paint around. Rags or natural sponges leave exact imprints, allowing the base color to come through. A vigorous dabbing with a dry, stiff brush held at right angles to the surface will give you an overall stippled finish that's ideal for small objects, mirror frames or door panels. If you find the varnish difficult to handle on larger areas, a little linseed oil will slow down the drying time and keep the mixture workable. The same principles can be used after stenciling to create a softer or antiqued effect.

The basic principles of broken color can be applied to make a wide variety of interesting effects. The different imprints left from sponges, rags or a dry brush all create perfect backgrounds for stenciling.

POSITIONING YOUR STENCIL

There is nothing worse than a stencil that is obviously supposed to be smack-dab in the middle of a surface and is obviously not. Similarly, a crooked motif or border that starts dropping halfway across a wall can make even grown men cry. Since you have been conscientious enough to find the middle of your design and provide yourself with a straight ruled midline, there should be no reason why you can't measure the surface and leave a light pencil mark to match up with the center mark of your stencil. For smaller flat surfaces, a triangle can be used to ensure the center line is a true right angle. Walls will need a level to give you a true vertical. Since the walls, ceilings and floors of many houses only closely approximate perfect right angles, use a level to make a line for a repeating border to follow.

One of the cardinal rules of stenciling is to always start in the middle and work outward. This ensures that the design is correctly balanced within the perimeters of the surface. If you have designed a repeating stencil to fit exactly from corner to corner, that's great. If not, then starting from the middle will mean that any funny little fractions or gaps are kept to the less visible perimeters.

You will now need to fix your stencil firmly in place. Small pieces of masking tape at each corner will hold it nice and steady—but try out the masking tape first to make sure it doesn't remove any of the existing surface paint. Thumbtacks leave permanent little holes. By far the best solution is spray

The center line of the stencil should always be aligned with a measured mark if the stencil is to fit a specific area.

Small pieces of masking tape can be used to hold the stencil in position—but try out the masking tape first to make sure it doesn't remove any existing surface paint.

adhesive, particularly the sort sold as temporary for mounting photographs. Be warned, however, that the spray can settle and stick to anything within range. It is also one of the nastiest things to inhale. So, provided that there isn't too much wind to blow dust and grit onto the sticky surface, it's best to spray outside. Go for a fine, even coat—the more glue you apply, the stickier it is and thus the more efficient it is at removing paint. The glue has a tendency to lose its tack as you go along, but try to resist the temptation to keep reapplying it. Technically, it is a good idea to remove glue from the stencil before reapplying, by rubbing it softly with a cotton ball and a little bit of lighter fluid. (But don't smoke.)

Spray adhesives will keep every bit of the stencil flat and fixed to the surface, and will ensure that you get crisp, high-definition stencils. They are great at holding delicate filaments in place, but you must be very gentle when peeling the stencil from the surface, to avoid damaging the finer cuts. Unfortunately, spray adhesives are not cheap, but you will find a can extremely useful for a variety of jobs around the home.

*For running patterns, it is
essential to mark out the
repeat before you start.*

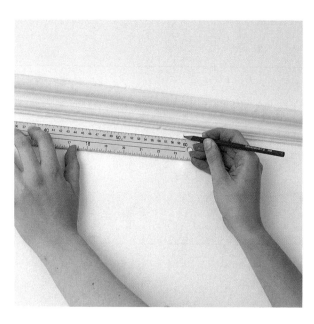

*Leave any half repeats
or corners until last to
minimize damage to the
stencil.*

APPLYING YOUR STENCIL

Having calculated where the stencil is to go and
how many times it is to repeat, make a mental note
of any halves or fractions of the design you will
need to fit into corners, around light fixtures, and
so on. Always make sure you have tackled every
inch of an area that takes a full repeat before
attempting to bend the stencil to fit into a corner
or around an impediment. Bending stencils not
only reduces their strength and life span, but can
also distort the design. Bending the design around
a corner is best done in two stages, with time
allowed for the first half to dry before applying the
stencil to the adjacent surface. You will be surprised
how much a corner will disguise inconsistencies or
botched repeats, provided the top and bottom correspond with the stencil levels on the adjacent surface.

Whether using a brush or a sponge, always
remove as much excess paint as possible before
setting to work. Thoroughly dab the paint onto a
piece of newspaper or an uncut part of the stencil
until you are left with a crisp, clear imprint of your
brush or your sponge. Then, starting in the middle
of the largest cut, work back so that by the time you
get to the edges, a minimal amount of paint is being
applied. (Fuzzy edges and trickles occur when too
much paint builds up at the edge of the cut.) If the
design is beginning to look a little faint by the time
you get to the edges, don't worry; you can always
go back over it with subsequent, light layers. But
you will be amazed at how visible and crisp the final
effect will be once you have removed the stencil.
Keeping your brush at right angles to the surface is
essential. If it's at an angle, you will find that stray
hairs can easily sneak behind the stencil and mark the
wall. Keep a small dish or saucer of water and lots
of cleaning fluids on hand. If you have small
smudges or dribbles, timely application with a
cotton ball may be enough to save the day. Often,
however, you may find you have to resign yourself
to painting out mistakes with a fine brush when
the stenciled project is complete and dry.

SPRAY STENCILING

In most cases when spray stenciling, you will have to mask surrounding areas to protect them from the spray. This can often mean you end up working "blind," as registration or center marks can be difficult to see. Spray stenciling is a lot more complicated to set up than other techniques, though spraying the paint makes up for lost time in preparation. As with brushed or sponged stencils, any buildup of paint near the edge can lead to drops or dribbles, so keep your spray as fine as possible.

If you are planning to reuse a stencil, always make sure it is stored flat. After a heavy-duty session, stencils can end up quite soggy. Spray-mounting them on glass or ceramic will hold them flat as they dry off and will make them easy to remove when dry. Excess paint should be carefully wiped off before storage; a light dusting of talcum powder will absorb any excess moisture.

VARNISHING

The durability of any stenciling project is greatly increased by a coat or two of varnish. Though not really necessary over a high-level border stenciled on top of latex, varnishing is essential on anything that might receive heavy wear or regular use. On aesthetic grounds, a coat of varnish will make colors richer and more attractive. High-gloss finishes should, for the most part, be avoided in favor of satin varnishes. Both finishes are available in polyurethane or acrylic (water-soluble). Polyurethane and acrylic are both equally good, though, despite what it says on the can, polyurethane is not entirely clear and will yellow the stencil slightly. This can often be a bonus in that it will take the edge off bright colors and build a little age into the finish. You could take this further still by adding a little oil paint (any of the umbers or siennas work beautifully), well diluted with turpentine, to the varnish. This will give you a glaze, which you can rub with a stiff, dry brush before the glaze

dries totally, to achieve a thoroughly lived-in finish.

Purists will want to gently sand each coat of varnish with fine sandpaper and build up a series of thin varnish coats. This will get rid of any dust or tiny grit particles that have managed to lodge in the wet varnish. Always stir varnish thoroughly before use, because it can settle if left too long on the shelf. Short strokes with a slightly upright brush will give you a more consistent finish. Again, aim for several thin coats rather than a thick layer, which could eventually crack or become discolored.

Smudged stencils are caused by a buildup of paint at the edges. You can avoid this by starting in the middle of each element and gradually working outward.

Projects

With your newly acquired stenciling skills, you'll find all the projects that follow easy to make. But don't forget, they are just ideas. Each of the stencil designs featured can be used on absolutely anything you like—just scale them up or down as required. You will be amazed at the results you can achieve!

Mirror frame

You will need:

- Mirror frame of unvarnished, untreated wood
- Fine sandpaper
- Eggshell latex in pale stone color
- Pencil
- Ruler
- Oil board, acetate or tracing paper
- X-Acto knife and cutting mat
- Spray adhesive
- Yellow Ochre acrylic paint
- Bowl or saucer (for mixing paints)
- Sponge
- Clear polyurethane varnish

For oil-primed surfaces
- Alkyd, craft spray or oil paint
- Mineral spirits (for cleaning brushes)

This is an excellent project for beginners, since it's quick and easy to make. Our starting point was a very simple mirror frame of untreated pine. For such a down-to-earth object, we decided to utilize the rough finish of stenciling to create a rustic or "countrified" look.

Before buying the mirror, we checked to be sure that it hadn't been treated or varnished in any way—a varnished wood frame would need more complicated preparation (see p. 35). The frame was lightly sanded first to remove any roughness. Two

coats of eggshell latex were then applied, followed by some more latex mixed with a tint of Yellow Ochre acrylic paint. This new color was applied in a thin wash and gently rubbed to achieve a subtle clouded finish (see p. 34).

While the paint was drying, a classic ivy leaf design was drawn up. The simple outline of the ivy leaf was ideal for a stencil, and the long, undulating stalks were perfect for decorating tall, narrow areas. The position of each leaf and the regular curves of the stalks were carefully calculated to fit into the rectangular frame. After measuring the distance between the leaves and sketching in the stalks, a template was then cut directly from the outline of the leaf. The template was then drawn around to make the design.

The design was stenciled using a sponge. The chosen color had a base of acrylic Yellow Ochre to which some of the original latex had been added, to create a closely related, mellow color balance. After stenciling, the stencil was left to dry, then flipped over to create a mirror image. After a good 12 hours, a couple of coats of satin varnish were used to protect the paint.

1 *After applying a base coat, mix a little Yellow Ochre with the latex and apply to the frame with a sponge.*

2 *Lay out the stencil design, using an ivy leaf template. Divide the length of the mirror frame by the length of a leaf and stalk to calculate the number of leaves and stalks that will fit. Then draw around each ivy leaf template, and connect each leaf by drawing a curved line for the ivy stalk.*

3 *Apply Yellow Ochre acrylic through the cut stencil with a sponge.*

Monogrammed box

You will need:
- Box made of untreated wood, treated with dark oak–tinted varnish
- Dark oak–tinted varnish
- Brush
- Tracing paper
- Pencil
- Piece of string
- Ruler
- Pushpin
- Selected capital letters for monogram, cut out from a newspaper
- Oil board, acetate or tracing paper
- X-Acto knife and cutting mat
- Spray adhesive
- Yellow Ochre and Dark Umber craft spray
- Pinking shears
- Mineral spirits (for cleaning brushes)

For oil-primed surfaces
- Alkyd, craft spray or oil paint
- Mineral spirit (for cleaning brushes)

This is an ideal personalized present—particularly appropriate as a wedding gift, since the initials of the couple can be combined in the monogram. The starting point was a very ordinary little box to which a few coats of dark oak–colored varnish had been applied.

The first thing to do was to make an accurate diagram of the box lid and then to calculate its center by joining each corner from the diagonal. With the midpoint calculated, a makeshift compass using a piece of string and a pushpin gave a perfect circle. If you do this, remember to keep the string as taut as possible. Make sure you leave a little space around the circle so that the design is not cramped on the box lid.

The next stage was to make the monogram, since the size and shape of the letters would affect the size and shape of the border. The letters H and S were traced from a newspaper headline, and their size slightly increased with a photocopier. (The more the letters are interwoven, the more decorative the monogram will become.) Because the box lid was quite small, simple classic letters were used, but they were made more interesting by making the S curve and snake around the straight lines of the H.

A wreathed circle of reeds and long, pointed leaves was chosen for the border. First, a rough sketch was made, following one-half of the circle drawn earlier. Then, when the right look was achieved, the half was reversed to finish the circle and make a symmetrical, perfectly balanced wreath.

A light spray in a Gold Ochre color was then applied. Craft spray was chosen for this project because of its suitability for a varnished surface, but a box with a base coat of latex obviously offers more flexibility in terms of choice of paint. Because the desired finish was one similar to marquetry, in which different wood veneers are used to make patterns, a gently broken layer of a Dark Umber color was then sprayed on to create a wood grain effect.

1 Make an accurate diagram of the top of the box and find its midpoint by connecting the diagonals from each corner. Using a piece of string and a pushpin as shown to create a simple compass, create a circle from the midpoint of the box.

2 Take chosen initials and enlarge them to the required size (see p. 24). Combine them on tracing paper to form your decorative monogram. Then, following the circle in step 1, draw up one side of the wreath border, using tracing paper to create a mirror image.

The finished stencil now had a richness and depth to it, but the motif seemed rather isolated. So a pretty border detail was created to edge the perimeter of each side by cutting masks, then using pinking shears to cut a zigzag border $\frac{1}{8}$ to $\frac{1}{4}$ inch (3 to 6mm) in from each edge. The masking required in such cases is time-consuming—particularly since each face can only be sprayed when the previous stencil is dry—but the effect is well worth it. To unify the effect and give further depth to the gold-colored stencil, the finished box was then given a final coat of the tinted satin varnish originally applied as a base coat on the box.

3 *Having combined the border and the monogram, transferred them to oiled paper and cut the stencil, mark all areas of the box you are not spraying, and apply a thin coat of Yellow Ochre craft spray. Let it dry, then spray a second gentle application of Dark Umber, allowing the paint to spatter.*

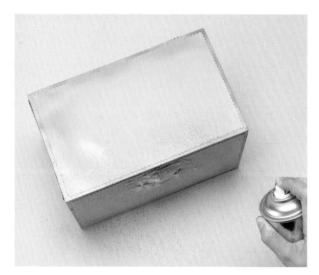

4 *Create a sawtooth border on your stencil with pinking shears, and allow the box to dry for a few hours.*

5 *Apply a final coat of the dark oak–colored varnish used to treat the box originally.*

R *epeating border*

You will need:

- An "egg and dart" design, with at least 4 eggs and 4 darts
- Level
- Tracing paper
- Pencil
- Tape measure
- Oil board, acetate or tracing paper
- X-Acto knife and cutting mat
- Warm gray acrylic paint mixed with a little latex
- Brushes
- Flake White acrylic paint
- Clear polyurethane varnish

This decorative border is designed to look like a dado—an architectural device used up until early this century to protect wall finishes from the damage caused by chair backs. Dados offer many design possibilities, since they can add detail to an otherwise plain room, and can be used to improve the proportions of a low-ceilinged, square space. The traditional height of a dado, based on classical architecture, is exactly one-third of the overall height of a room. You can, however, play around with this proportion to suit yourself. Very low-ceilinged rooms will seem much higher with a dado

a little on the low side, and a high ceiling can be brought down with a tall dado.

The design chosen to define this dado was a simplified "egg and dart" motif frequently used by wallpaper companies for borders. Its close repeat means that awkward corners, such as those around a fireplace, can be easily accommodated without any obvious missed or botched repeats. The design itself was traced from a book of classical architectural moldings, then photocopied to a size that worked well within the space—in this case, 2 inches (5cm) high. Before marking a line around

1 Trace your design carefully and shade in the "negative" areas between each egg and dart.

the room, however, the chosen height was checked to see that it cleared the top of any radiators, to allow plenty of room for a clear, crisp finish. The dado line should also not be so high that it passes over the mantel, or directly over the windows.

Coming up with the right dimensions involves a lot of experimentation that, when it comes down to it, is best done visually, without measuring. Using a level, a faint pencil line was marked around the area to be stenciled, and the height checked every now and then with a tape measure.

Taking the original traced section, which had

2 Mark a line around the room using a level. Gently apply warm gray acrylic through the stencil. Allow it to dry for a few seconds before applying a second layer at the top of the stencil.

four eggs and four corresponding darts, a separate trace was made with two parallel lines defining the perimeter of the design. This was laid over the original. Having measured the width of the eggs and the darts, right-angled sections between the two lines were then marked. (For this alternate repeat, it is essential that if you start with an egg at one end, you finish with a dart at the other.)

This stencil is what's known as "reversed." In other words, the design has been used to define the area between the eggs and the darts, to give the motif a more three-dimensional look. The straight upper and lower edge also prevents it from looking messy or isolated on the wall.

The close repeat of the design meant it wasn't really necessary to start in the middle of the wall when applying the stencil. A warm gray was mixed with some of the background color of the wall to add a three-dimensional effect, and finished with the same paint as the surrounding wall. Using a stiff, dry brush, latex was applied along the stencil, leaving as light a finish as possible. The latex dried in about 5 minutes, which meant we could then go back to the beginning of each stencil and apply more paint to the top of each cut. This gave a flat, darker area, which, when the stencil was removed, looked like shadows between the mouldings.

For the highlight color, some of the original wall latex was mixed with some Flake White acrylic containing just a dash of complementary red. Working diagonally from bottom right to top left, less and less paint was left on the wall. A final coat of satin varnish was then applied for added protection.

3 Cut a second stencil the same shape as the egg, but about ¼ inch (6mm) smaller all the way round. Then, using a dry brush with some Flake White acrylic, highlight the bottom right corner with a dry brush dipped in white acrylic.

The completed border.

The bedroom

This stenciled bedroom shows just how wonderfully flexible stenciling can be. The design is a particularly pretty modern version of the French eighteenth-century pattern known as "Toile de Jouy." It is an intricate and delicate pattern, but the strong lines and emphatic shapes, together with the variety of separate motifs, have a great deal of scope.

The original idea was to just focus on the headboard—and possibly the cupboards—and leave the rest to evolve naturally. This is often the best approach, since it means that options can be kept open and decisions made on the spur of the moment. Patterned areas can then be easily balanced with undecorated finishes in the space, and a scheme

Headboard

1 Calculate the central mark of the headboard and the central line of the stencil. Suspend a pencil from a piece of string from the central mark of the headboard, then offset the stencil from this central mark and apply warm gray acrylic using a sponge. When dry, realign the central line of the stencil to the central mark of the headboard, and apply terracotta latex with a sponge.

2 Notice how effective using the same stencil twice can be in adding depth to the design.

created from different elements unified by color and pattern.

The first point of attack was the headboard. Its central point was calculated, and, using a makeshift plumb line made from a piece of string and a pencil, gravity gave us a "true vertical" center line. A mental note was then made of how high the pillows came—losing the very end of a design behind pillows looks nice and informal, but to mislay more than 40 percent under linen would look messy. This particular headboard was made by cutting a piece of medium-density fiberboard into a shape that perfectly complemented the motif. The headboard was then screwed straight into the plaster and given the same paint treatment as the rest of the wall. In this case, it was latex, but if you are about to stencil an existing headboard, chances are that it will be finished in an oil paint, for which you will need to use a spray.

The stencil was aligned with the center mark, then moved about $\frac{1}{8}$ inch (3mm) to the left and a little down. To add more interest to the design, a "drop shadow" effect was created by a light sponge application of a pale warm gray. When this had completely dried, the design was stenciled in a terracotta latex to go with the fabric. By realigning this stencil to the center line, the terracotta motif was then centered to the headboard.

The large design here offered plenty of scope for a wide range of techniques. Different densities of paint add interest and life to a pattern, and a few minutes spent sharpening some of the shapes with a fine paintbrush will leave you with a polished finish. Varnishing is essential on a headboard because it is exposed not only to knocks and scrapes, but also oily heads. In this case, a little Yellow Ochre was added to the varnish for a mellow antique effect.

A smaller version of the central design was used to add interest to the bedside tables, and the larger version with a spray was used on the lampshades. For the rather plain cupboards, the pretty jug motif

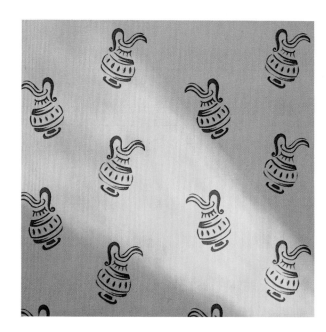

Cupboards

Stenciling an entire wall to look like wallpaper requires a lot of preliminary measuring. Using a plumb line or level, divide the area vertically. The effect works best when, as here, the motif is alternately reversed.

from the headboard design was isolated and photocopied until it was small enough to fit. The cupboards had been finished in eggshell paint, and as we wanted to stencil directly onto the cupboards, we had to mix up a new color in an oil paint. Alkyd was used because it dries more quickly and has a stiffer texture than ordinary oil-based paints. The original acrylic color used for the headboard was based on an earthy red. (You will find that acrylic and oil paints have many colors in common, which means that different surfaces can have the same colored stencil.)

There was no pre-set plan for how many jug motifs would be used over the cupboards, or where they would be placed. Having come to the end, there was one jug too many—but, since it had only recently been applied, it was easily removed with a rag soaked in turpentine.

Decorative frieze

You will need:

- Tracing paper
- Pencil
- Oil board, acetate or tracing paper
- X-Acto knife and cutting mat
- Spray adhesive
- Bowl or saucer (for mixing paints)
- Grayish yellow, dark pink, dusky pink and green-gray latex paint
- Sponge
- Level

This project helps solve one of the most common problems encountered by the interior designer: the contrast between richly colored and patterned fabrics and a pale-colored wall. Often, the patterned fabric of curtains is the only one in the room, so these colors and design need to be carried through to create a more integrated feel to the space. This is best achieved with a stenciled border, or frieze, running below the cornice.

The color choices for the stencil were relatively easy: grayish yellow, dark pink, light pink and greenish gray. At first sight, however, the pattern seemed to offer too many choices. Although charming, the small curtain motif was too complicated for stenciling; the elongated wreath with its stylized bows was too tall and thin to act as a border, and the fruit bowl, in its entirety, was too busy for a repeated design. The upper half of the fruit bowl, on the other hand, immediately caught the eye as a good starting point for the border. So this element was traced. The grapes, however,

were left out, as they would end up looking too dense. This left a rather noticeable gap in the bottom right-hand corner, which was filled by repeating a few of the flowers from the top of the design. The design now seemed too square, so the elegant curved bow was lifted from the adjacent motif. The end result was something that was not only attractive, but perfect for a repeating pattern. The shapes were simplified slightly, the filaments sketched in, and the whole thing photocopied several times.

Although this is a four-color design, only three separate stencils were used. (If you work cleanly and methodically, there is no limit to the amount of color you can use through one stencil.) Like all furnishing fabrics, this fabric had a series of small color registration circles showing each of the colors used to make up the design—a helpful guide when mixing paints. (If you hunt around inside your curtains, you will probably find them on an outside seam.) In this case, the elegant grayish yellow

1 The starting point for the stencil design.

2 Having traced and adapted the fruit bowl motif, add adjacent elements to round off the design.

3 Mix up the tints, referring to the fabric and the color registration marks on the back of the fabric. Try out each color on the background wall color and let it dry.

color in the curtains formed the starting point. This was the base color from which the other colors were created. The grayish yellow base was put into three containers. To the first were added carefully controlled dribbles of a dusky pink; to the second, gray-green; and to the third, a tiny amount of a wine-colored paint.

All the colors were then put on a photocopy of the design and matched up in different combinations to suit the different elements in the pattern. The zigzagging lines that followed the contours of the motif to soften changes from color to color in the original fabric were retained for the stencil. In the curtains, some of the pattern elements, such as the rim of the grapefruit, the highlights on the apple and the leaves, were created by leaving the light base color blank. Since light stenciling allows much of the base color to show through, additional shades can be created by applying one color onto another. Therefore, areas where the green and the pink could be made lighter by being applied over the pale wall color were marked.

4 Color in the final photocopy of the design.

5 Trace the outline of each color on a separate piece of tracing paper.

The final design was then broken down into three color stencils by tracing the outline of each area of color, ensuring that the center lines were accurately marked on each trace.

The first stencil was used for the grayish yellow color. The areas where the wall color was to be used were clearly marked. (If oil board is used, make a V-shaped groove at either side along the horizontal midpoint.) A line was then drawn with a level to follow. At the midpoint of each wall, the position of each stenciled repeat was then marked off, so that we could see where to bend the design to fit around corners.

After finishing the first stencil, the registration grooves were followed with a light pencil line. The other stencils were lined up on these marks, and the pencil lines were removed with an eraser.

6 To see if the finished effect works, try each stencil out on a piece of paper before applying it to the wall.

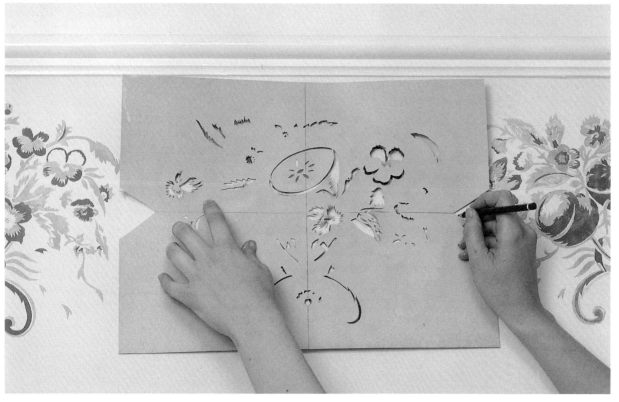

7 To ensure that each stencil is correctly registered, cut V-shaped grooves along the center line of each. Make a light pencil mark on these V grooves and then line up each subsequent stencil to the mark.

Stenciled stripes

You will need:
- Level
- Pencil
- Eraser
- Low-tack masking tape or oil board
- Spray adhesive
- Calculator
- Triangle
- Clear polyurethane varnish
- Linseed oil
- Raw Umber oil paint
- 2 brushes—1 wet, 1 dry
- Turpentine or mineral spirits (for cleaning brushes)

Unusual wall finishes below a dado are both popular and extremely effective. Using broadly striped wall papers below dado rails was very common during much of the nineteenth century, and this effect can be easily reproduced with paint. Vertical stripes are an effective device for increasing the height of a room, but can sometimes be a little too bold if used over an entire wall. Restricted to the area below a dado rail, however, they add a note of elegance and increase the feeling of space without overpowering the rest of the scheme.

Dados are often largely obscured by furniture, which means you can afford to be quite daring in your color combinations if you are striving for a very contemporary look. For this project, however, the colors were kept muted and tonally balanced for a classically elegant look.

Although the following method of painting stripes is not stenciling in its purest form, it uses the same principles. If you have no architectural dado moulding, you will have to draw a level line to work to. You will also eventually need to use either a printed paper border or repeating stencil to create a neat finishing line for the stripes. The "egg and dart" decorative border (see p. 47) is ideal for neatly finishing painted stripes.

Technically speaking, spending some time and effort calculating a stripe that will fit exactly on each wall should be the first step, but this process involves some rather complicated calculations. We felt that since our stripes were in such a subtle shade, they could accommodate being split on corners, though a bolder combination of colors where the stripes are very defined might need greater consideration.

The easiest stripes are those that are equidistant, or that have the same width for both the stripe and the space between.

A level was taken around the room to measure heights and levels, after which a piece of cardboard was cut to the width and height of the stripes—it's very important, in such instances, that all the corners are right-angled, so using a triangle is a good idea. This piece was then used as a template to mark the stripes around the room, starting from the middle of the wall we felt was most visible. A level was used every now and then to check that the stripes were vertical. Since dark or heavy pencil lines would inevitably show through the finished stripes, minimum pressure was applied with a hard pencil, leaving as pale a mark as possible. A piece of paper, cut to shape and held in place with spray adhesive, could be used as a mask, though in this case low-tack masking tape was used—trimmed in half so as not to obscure adjacent stripes. Ordinary masking tape, whatever the manufacturers may claim, can be very good at pulling off existing

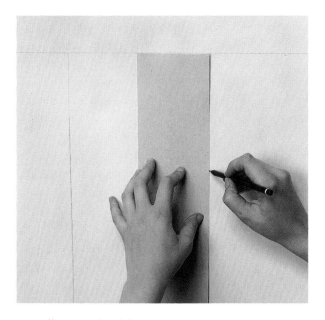

1 Following a level line, mark the position of each stripe using a cardboard template.

paintwork. Low-tack masking tape is not difficult to find, and is not only reusable, but also very easy to put on in a straight line.

An oil-based glaze was used, together with half a small container of satin varnish with a dash of linseed oil, and some Raw Umber dissolved in turpentine. Latex could obviously be used, but if, as here, you want to disguise a radiator in the paint scheme, you will need to use oil paint or spray. No amount of coaxing will keep latex on a radiator for long.

Having masked a few stripes, the glaze was applied working from the middle of the stripe outward, so that the brush was drier as it hit the tape. Because a slow-drying oil glaze was used, the stripe had to be gone over again with a coarse, dry brush, literally dragging the paint downward, keeping the brush at a right angle to the wall. The result was lovely mellow stripes with a delicately "worn" texture to them. You could, however, successfully use other techniques with rags, sponges or plastic bags to create a texture in the paint. (If, when you remove the tape or the paper mask, you find the glaze has seeped underneath and smudged, speedy action with a cotton ball soaked in turpentine will save the day.)

It's always a good idea to start painting in an area that you know will be hidden by a sofa or in a dark corner behind your stereo. This will give you an opportunity to gain confidence before tackling the more visible areas, such as alcoves on either side of the fireplace.

Because a varnish-based glaze was used on this project, an additional coat of varnish was not needed. But bear in mind that latex stripes are easily scuffed unless they are sealed with a tough satin varnish.

Stenciled stripes—perfect for below a dado rail.

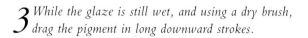
2 Mask the edge of each stripe using either low-tack masking tape or oil board and spray adhesive. Apply the varnish/pigment glaze in short diagonal strokes.

3 While the glaze is still wet, and using a dry brush, drag the pigment in long downward strokes.

The nursery

You will need:
- Oil board, acetate or tracing paper
- X-Acto knife and cutting mat
- Spray adhesive
- Scrap paper for masking
- Craft spray or acrylic paints in assorted colors
- Permanent marker
- Pen
- Masking tape

Of all the rooms in the house, the stenciled nursery has become an enduring favorite. This is probably due to the fact that nursery stencils at their best are simple and bright. Although complicated stencil schemes, such as locomotives accurately reproduced down to the last piston, are undeniably lovely, it's a matter of debate whether such sophistication is appreciated by the room's tiny inhabitants. It's a depressing fact of life that within a few frighteningly short years, anything you stencil in the nursery will be dismissed by its occupant as being for "babies." So, while the children are still young and without the necessary vocabulary to complain, go for bright saturated colors, which tiny, new-formed eyes do seem to notice and enjoy.

Most nurseries are furnished during the month-by-month countdown to the new arrival, which means that particular attention must be paid to the

1 Connect the top and bottom of a center line to form a curved balloon shape, then cut the stencil. Make sure that before spraying through the stencil onto the wall, the surrounding area has been completely masked.

2 When the base color has dried, spurt-spray a second color by taping a pin to the side of the can so that it interrupts the spray of paint.

3 A short burst from the white spray gives a lifelike highlight. Draw in the curling balloon string using a black permanent marker.

The balloon shape used could not be easier—a suitable curve joins the top and bottom of a center line, which is then traced to provide a symmetrical mirror image. By keeping the paint spray fine, the stencil is quite transparent, allowing the overlap between the two balloons to create a new color. The same effects are possible with a dry application of latex or acrylic paint.

To give the balloons added interest and life, a contrast color was "spurt"-sprayed. (Basically, this means taping a pin or needle to the top of the can so that it directly interrupts the spray of paint, resulting in larger blobs and spots of color.) A white spray was then used to create a highlight that made the balloons look round and rubbery. The curving, curling strings were added with a square-nibbed permanent marker.

The metal toy chest was first sprayed a sky blue color, then the fluffy clouds were sprayed on through a simple cloud-shaped stencil. To add a little more depth, some of the clouds received the lightest possible spray, while others took several coats to make them dense. For a really airy effect, the same principle could be applied to the walls. Start with a blue latex that has a faint suggestion of violet, and vary the denseness and size of the clouds by spraying only the edge of the stencil on some of them to give a real feeling of space.

This type of random project is ideal for tackling a little at a time. More than one nursery has remained incomplete after the arrival of its new occupant, as the task became an increasing burden to the heavily pregnant stenciler. The beauty of this scheme is that there is no definite end to it— you could find balloons appearing anywhere!

dangers of paint fumes and ladders. The nursery shown here is bold, simple and designed in such a way that it can be completed over an extended period. In order for the stencil to be applied over a variety of surfaces with little time-consuming preparation, craft sprays have been used. This means that proper ventilation and a good face mask are essential. It may also be a good idea to quickly check with the manufacturers about safety. Although craft sprays are not theoretically harmful, car sprays could be potentially very dangerous if you are pregnant.

The kitchen

You will need:
- Oil board, acetate or tracing paper
- X-Acto knife and cutting mat
- Spray adhesive
- Sponge
- Acrylic paints in assorted colors
- Heat-resistant varnish
- Paintbrush
- Mineral spirits (for cleaning brush)
- Saucer (for mixing paints)

After the rather clinical-looking kitchens of the last decade, it's been a relief to see a friendlier look resurfacing in recent kitchen designs. One of the problems is that since wallpaper is rarely advisable in an area where steam and heat are constantly produced, the potential for introducing pattern and accents of color in a kitchen using conventional methods is quite limited. This makes the durable finish of stenciling ideal for adding some life and interest to this room. Having said that, however, it must also be said that kitchen stencils must be limited to surfaces that are receptive to paint if you want the designs to survive. There is no paint in the world that will continue to look good and still adhere to modern laminates, and painting on ceramic tiles should only be attempted with special tile paint, which is too runny for stenciling. Wood

kitchen cabinets will, however, take stenciled designs that will endure most things if properly varnished. If, as here, your cabinet fronts are laminated, however, concentrate instead on stenciling the door panels or walls.

The stenciled kitchen chosen here uses an appropriately culinary stencil with a bold outline and simple shapes that are in keeping with the countrified feel of the room. The form of each object is boldly blocked in with a rough-textured application of paint using a dryish sponge.

When completely dry, the detail is added freehand with a paintbrush. This may sound daunting, but is, in fact, less complicated than cutting a series of different stencils for each color. As long as you take time to create a prototype to follow, as with the frieze (see p. 53), you can't go wrong. The

1 Cut the outline shape of the stencil design, and apply a textured coat of pale ochre acrylic paint.

rustic look of this design is actually improved by irregularity and roughness.

Stencils used on a kitchen wall should always be varnished. Here, the stenciled baskets have received several coats of varnish to protect them, and the stencil design on the tray has been treated with a heat-resistant varnish to protect it from hot mugs or plates.

As in the nursery and bedroom, this scheme benefits from an "organic" approach that offers tremendous freedom for the stenciler. By varying the scale of the motif to correspond with the object to be stenciled, the design can crop up anywhere and allows for a series of small-scale, quick projects.

2 Following your prototype on cardboard, tint the various different elements in the design using watered-down acrylic paints over the original stencil.

3 Apply several coats of heat-resistant varnish to anything that may come in contact with hot plates or mugs.

The stenciled kitchen.

A Mexican-style bathroom

You will need:
- Oil board, acetate or tracing paper
- X-Acto knife and cutting mat
- Pencil
- Tracing paper
- Coarse sandpaper
- Spray adhesive
- Acrylic paints in assorted colors
- Warm terracotta flat latex
- Satin spray varnish
- Clear polyurethane varnish
- Newspaper

Bathrooms are best approached with a degree of whimsy and fun. Usually tiny, they are rarely of any architectural merit and are inhabited for only a limited time each day. Many bathrooms, as here, can have a very cold feel, due to large expanses of shiny white ceramic and direct overhead lighting. A strong—perhaps even daring—approach to color offers instant improvement and an ideal opportunity to explore a particular theme.

In this bathroom, the bright warm colors and primitive patterns of Mexico have been used as a starting point. The architecture in this space is so disjointed that the mellow terracotta finish has been extended to the ceiling to create a feeling of warmth and color. The bold wall and ceiling Zigarat stencils have been "weathered" by rubbing with a coarse-grain sandpaper, and the surfaces have been varnished for extra protection.

Thinned-down latex was rubbed into the grain of the untreated wooden shelf, which was suspended from the ceiling to clear the sloping wall in this attic room. Additional detail was provided by upholstery tacks. The stenciled motif was kept as rough as possible, in colors derived from the Mexican pottery on the shelves.

The colorful collection of terracotta flowerpots was stenciled with brightly hued acrylic paints. They could just as easily have been hand-painted, since acrylics have the advantage of drying quickly. They are also opaque enough to cover up mistakes or changes. Having given the pots a latex finish, a large cone shape was made with a piece of newspaper. The flowerpot was then placed inside, and the top and the bottom of the pot traced with a felt-tip pen. By carefully undoing the cone, a template was left that fitted the flowerpot snugly. The stencil was taken from this shape.

It's far easier, when stenciling a curved and tapering object, to make a stencil that fits like a glove in this way—it means that the paint is less likely to smudge or seep. After a little freehand detailing and a couple of coats of gloss varnish, these pots look just like Mexican ceramics. But bear in mind that they will be unlikely to survive very long outside without several coats of spar varnish.

The stenciled window solves a common problem. In bathrooms, it's a good idea to have glass that lets in light, but is still opaque enough to

Walls *Having color-washed the walls with a terracotta flat latex, apply the Zigarat and star stencil with a sponge, using an opaque layer of the background wall color between the surface. Rub the surface with coarse-grain sandpaper.*

prevent you from being seen. Obscure, or textured, glass is rarely attractive, and sandblasted glass is very expensive. On the other hand, car spray, when sprayed directly onto glass, gives it a real sandblasted effect. It is also durable and practical enough for most windows.

For this window, a variety of star shapes were cut, together with the Mexican Zigarat. The window frame was masked, and the motifs stuck to the glass with spray adhesive. The window was then gently sprayed (you will need to wear a mask for this, as the fumes are particularly unpleasant). This technique can be used for a variety of applications. If you prefer a Victorian-inspired bathroom, ordinary paper doilies will give a

lacelike finish, while leaves attached to the glass with white glue will give you a ready-made forest glade.

Panes of glass and mirrors can be bordered by simply using masking tape and a straight line. For example, a particularly elegant window above a front door can be stenciled with the number of the house.

To do this, simply trace the existing brass number from the front door and make a mask from oil board. Then use a masking tape border to create a clear frame around the pane. One of the joys of this technique is that when direct sunlight streams straight through the stenciled glass, the unsprayed areas creating the motif are projected perfectly onto the opposite wall.

Shelf *Apply thinned-down latex straight onto the grain of the untreated wood, and stencil over it using bright primitive colors.*

Household items *Many interesting effects can be achieved by using a variety of household items as a mask for your spray stencil pattern. Use paper doilies* *for lacelike effects, leaves for a forest glade—even large paper clips can create interesting effects.*

Pots *Make a large cone shape from a sheet of newspaper, scrap paper or tracing paper. Follow the top and bottom edges of the flowerpot with a pencil. Carefully unwrap the paper, and you will have an exact template of the flowerpot from which you can derive your stencil.*

Window *By using spray varnish, various effects similar to sandblasted glass can be achieved on windows. This is an easy-* *to-achieve and good-looking alternative to textured or opaque glass bathroom windows.*

*G*ift *ideas*

You will need:

Wrapping paper
- Brown paper
- Gold craft spray
- Glitter spray
- Oil board, acetate or tracing paper
- X-Acto knife and cutting mat
- Lightweight card stock for gift tags

Photograph frame and album
- Same for wrapping paper (except for glitter spray)
- Glue

Placemats
- Dense fiberboard
- Jigsaw
- White latex paint
- Pale blue acrylic paint
- Oil board, acetate or tracing paper
- X-Acto knife and cutting mat
- Acrylic varnish
- Blue carbon or transfer paper
- Soft pencil
- Fixative spray
- Heat-resistant varnish
- Blue felt
- White glue

There can be no doubt that actually making a Christmas or birthday present gives more satisfaction, and gains more Brownie points, than simply popping into the nearest department store. The flexibility of stenciling also means you can come up with a variety of gifts for very little money.

Wrapping paper *With the price of wrapping paper being so exorbitant, stenciling your own makes financial sense, as well as being great fun. It also means you can choose one particular color or design them, relating all the presents under your Christmas tree to that particular year's decoration. Here, ordinary brown paper has been used with spray stenciled stars. The gold craft spray used has been made even more twinkly by spraying glitter spray through the same stencil. (Glitter spray comes in a variety of finishes that are nonpermanent. It can be sprayed on Christmas trees or used on white linen tablecloths without permanently marking the fabric.) The coordinating gift tags have been mounted on lightweight card stock.*

Photograph album and frame *The photograph album itself has been covered in a heavy paper that was first stenciled and then varnished. This was very simple to do. First, the album was placed on the paper, then the sides, top and bottom of the paper were folded in. The corners were then cut away and two thin V-shaped grooves cut on either side of the spine. The cut corners of the cover were then stuck to each other.*

The same stencil used on the album cover has also been applied to a pre-cut picture frame bought at an art supply store, and bordered with a gold pen.

Wastepaper basket
- Wastebasket
- Oil board, acetate or tracing paper
- X-Acto knife and cutting mat
- High-gloss varnish tinted with Burnt Umber
- Raw Umber

Lampshade
- Lampshade
- Oil board, acetate or tracing paper
- X-Acto knife and cutting mat
- Oil paint
- Clear polyurethane varnish
- Soft thin brush with long bristles

Tablecloth
- Plain tablecloth
- Oil pastel colors
- Oil board, acetate or tracing paper
- X-Acto knife and cutting mat
- Spray adhesive

Fireplace screen
- Oil board, acetate or tracing paper
- X-Acto knife and cutting mat
- Chosen paints
- Spray adhesive

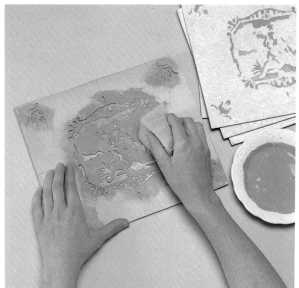

Placemats *The placemats were cut to size with a jigsaw from dense fiberboard and given several coats of white latex. A pale blue glaze was applied directly onto the base painting and, before it dried, was rubbed with a lightweight plastic bag. The subtle blue stencil was applied quite roughly. With blue carbon or transfer paper stuck to the back of the original drawing, the outlines and details were then traced with a thick, soft pencil. The mat was then sprayed with a fixative spray from an art supply store (though aerosol hairspray would do). Care had to be taken at this stage, since too much spray might have caused the carbon lines to bleed, so the applications were kept light and thin. A final coat of heat-resistant varnish and some blue felt, stuck to the reverse with white glue, finished the set of mats off perfectly.*

Wastepaper basket *The wooden wastepaper basket has been treated to an elegant new identity, inspired by eighteenth-century "Boulle-Work." Boulle-work, or brass and tortoiseshell decoration, was much prized as a rich finish for furniture in the eighteenth century. In this case, the basket was first sprayed with gold paint. A reverse stencil was then used to mask the metallic base color and a high-gloss varnish tinted with Burnt Umber applied over the exposed areas. While the varnish was still wet, patches of undiluted Raw Umber were worked in and the whole surface softly stroked with a dry brush to merge the pigment into the varnish. The gold base color shining through the translucent tinting creates a nice tortoiseshell effect.*

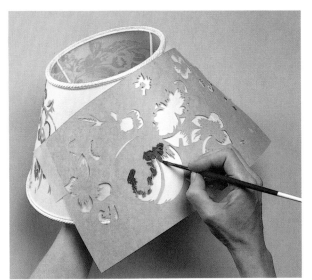

Fireplace screen *This is the* pièce de résistance. *It was cut from a sheet of medium-density fiberboard and stenciled with what must now be a familar design, enlarged by using a photo-copy machine. A little time was then spent finishing off the design with some free-hand detailing. Fireplace screens are an extremely attractive solution to a black, bare fireplace and were much loved in the eighteenth century. Here, a small, right-angled prop fixed to the back of the screen keeps it upright, and, as a final touch, a dark tinted varnish gives it a mellow antiqued finish.*

Lampshade *The lampshade stencil was cut using the same technique as on the flowerpots (p. 69), although this time, rather than stenciling the design, the cutout pattern was used as a guide for freehand painting. This meant that the motif could be done in oil paint mixed with a little varnish, which becomes transparent when light passes through it. Stenciling with oil and varnish onto paper or silk mounted on paper shades can end up being very messy. Use a soft brush with long bristles to ensure an even application of paint. Spray, acrylic and latex stencils can be used on lampshades, but will not give the same beautiful translucency as stencils using varnish and oil paint.*

Tablecloth *As a rule, stenciled fabrics are not entirely successful if they are frequently used or washed. This pretty cloth for a small table is unlikely to get much wear or get terribly dirty, so the first stencil from the book was used as a border. Rather than using conventional paint, which dries stiff on fabric, or expensive and difficult-to-find fabric paints, oil pastels from an art suply store were used. These give a very pleasant sketchy crayon effect that works very well on cotton. Since you will be rubbing the stencil quite hard with your crayon, you will need to stretch the fabric taut, and anchor the stencil firmly before starting; otherwise, the material may crease, leaving small lines in the design. The pastels can be made permanent on the cotton by ironing with a warm to hot iron through the back of the fabric onto a paper towel. This will melt and soak up the oil medium, leaving the pigment permanently in the fabric. Fabrics stenciled like this must not be dry-cleaned, but can be machine-washed on a cool setting.*

*T*emplates

Headboard (p. 50)

Headboard (p. 50)

Repeating border (p. 47)

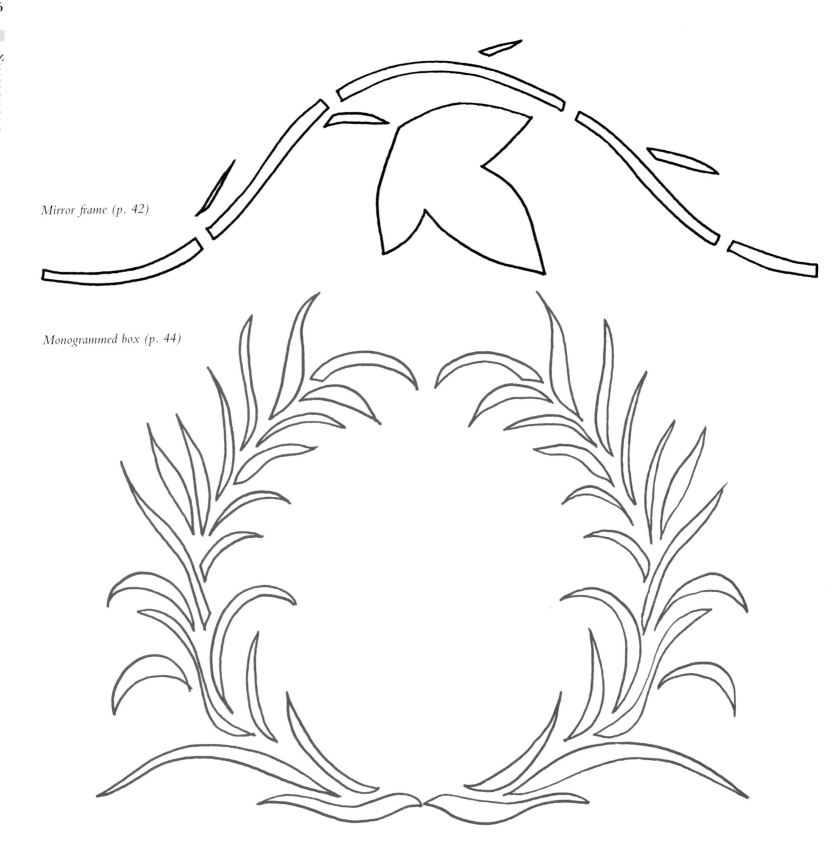

Mirror frame (p. 42)

Monogrammed box (p. 44)

Kitchen (p. 63) (reduced to 75%)

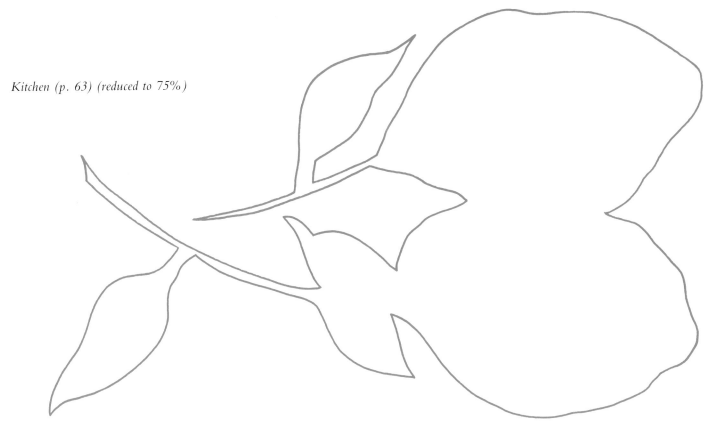

Gift ideas/wastepaper baskets (p. 72) (reduced to 75%)

Sources

Bentwood, Inc., P.O. Box 1676, Thomasville, GA 31792 (912) 226-1223. Shaker-style cheeseboxes, baskets, buckets, and canisters suitable for stenciling.

Adele Bishop Inc., P.O. Box 3349, Kingston, NC 28502-3349 (919) 527-4186. Pre-cut stencils, japan paints, brushes, knives, stencil sheets and instruction books.

Arthur Brown & Brothers, 2 West 46th Street, New York, NY 10036 (212) 575-5555. All stencil supplies, including pre-cut stencils, books, knives, paints and acetate.

Decorative Arts of Vermont, R.R. #1 Box 136, Dorset, VT 05251 (802) 867-5915. All stencil supplies, including pre-cut and ready-to-cut stencils, paints, brushes and knives.

Dover Publications, 31 E. 2nd Street, Mineola, NY 11501 (516) 294-7000. Publisher of a series of "cut & use" stencil books, printed on durable paper, including Pennsylvania Dutch, Art Nouveau, Victorian, Japanese, Art Deco and border designs. Write for free catalog.

A & A.J. Hutcheon, Inc., Artist Supplies, 92 Pleasant Street, Claremont, NH 03743 Attention: Charles Hutcheon (603) 542-5751. Clear acetate sheets, frosted Mylar sheets, Morilla stencil paper and oaktag, japan paints, knives and brushes.

Illinois Bronze Paint Co., Craft Finishes Division 300 E. Main Street, Lake Zurich, IL 60047. Pre-cut stencils, acrylic paints, fabric, paints, brushes.

Janovic Plaza, 1150 Third Avenue, New York NY 10021 (212) 722-1400. General paint and stenciling supplies.

Pavilion, 6a Howe Street, Edinburgh, Scotland; represented by Swift Morris Interiors, 1208 Washington Street, Hoboken, NJ 07030 (201) 656-5684. Pre-cut stencils.

Plaid Enterprises, 1649 International Boulevard, P.O. Drawer E, Norcross, GA 30091 (404) 923-8200. Pre-cut stencils, paints, brushes, books and stencil supplies.

Society for the Preservation of New England Antiquities, Harrison Gray Otis House, 141 Cambridge Street, Boston, MA 02114 (617) 227-3956. Moses Eaton stencil patterns, early American.

Stencil-Ease, P.O. Box 209, New Ipswich, NY 03071 (800) 633-5700. Large selection of pre-cut stencils, paints, brushes and kits.

Stencil World, 8 West 19th Street, New York, NY 10011. All stencil supplies, including pre-cut stencils, stencil patterns, instruction books, paints and brushes. Send $2.50 for catalog.

Index